About Us

JACK M OFFMAN, "BEST SELLING" AUTHOR

Jack M. Offman, the undiscovered gem of questionable children's novels, is a 40-something who finds joy in the nerdy realm of laser tag and video games—probably why he's still single. While his books might often get the silent treatment, he passionately dives into them after introspective beach walks and avoiding DUIs. And for the record, he's the kind of guy who'd never risk a sprint with scissors. Legends say his zest for life might just be infectious, if anyone bothered to listen.

AMANDA E TASS, WORLD'S MOST FIERY ILLUSTRATOR

Amanda E. Tass is a 30 somthing, flaming-haired tempest with a temper hotter than the sun's core. Trained in the dark arts of propaganda artistry, she wields her brush with the finesse of a sorceress, enchanting minds with her illustrations. Her secret techniques, whispered among the art elite, can make a skeptic believe in unicorns. Cross her, and you'll be begging for mercy faster than you can say "watercolor." With a black belt in Jiu Jitsu, she can flip you like a pancake and leave you feeling flatter than a canvas. Let's just say Amanda's fiery disposition didn't exactly open doors at more "respectable" publishing houses.

CLEVELAND STEAMER PRESS, TRASH BOOK PUBLISHER

Ah, Cleveland Steamer Press – surprisingly not from Cleveland and inspired by something so unsavory, we dare not speak its name. This publishing marvel somehow attracts authors even a garbage disposal might reject. Continually defying economic logic (never having turned a profit), this powerhouse pumps out "children's books" so dubious they're on society's blacklist. Truly, their books are best reserved for foes – consider them a paperweight with a vendetta.

CHRISTMAS Hand Jobs
FOR THE WHOLE FAMILY

- THE BOOK OF HOUSEHOLD FUN - HOURS OF HANDHELD ACTIVITIES - GREAT FOR ALL AGES -

BY
JACK M OFFMAN
AMANDA E TASS

ClevelandSteamerPress.com

Disclaimer

Preface

WHY WE LOVE HAND JOBS!

Welcome to "Christmas Hand Jobs for the Whole Family!" Whether you have enjoyed our previous volumes or are a hand jobs novice, we're thrilled to have you! This new volume continues to celebrate the joy of hands-on activities. From the practicality of emptying your sack to the delight of good stocking stuffing, this new book is designed to inspire creativity and foster hand-inspired holiday bonding. So, roll up your sleeves and dive into a world where your hands are not just appendages, but tools for crafting holiday experiences!

Trim the Tree

ERECT AND ENHANCE YOUR SEASONAL SPRUCE

Ready to trim your tree this holiday season? The last thing you want is for people to think you have an overgrown bush! Yuck! Keeping your tree nice and tidy makes it a great hand job and much easier to handle when erecting and adding delicate ornaments. Make sure it's a group activity, and let others fondle your blue balls! As you climb up to reach the top, it's crucial to cover the tip nicely. Once you've got it covered, you'll feel like a star, turning everyone on with those twinkly lights!

Get Knocked Up

KNOCK, KNOCK. WHO'S COMING?

Ready to get knocked up this holiday season? It's time to install a door knocker! Measure, mark, and drill pilot holes before gently nailing it in. Don't forget to drill a peephole, so you can see who's coming for your big spread. Whether you prefer big, hard-to-miss knockers, ones that hang, or small, playful ones, everyone will want to get handsy with yours after this banging hand job!

Stuffing the Turkey

START YOUR FEAST WITH A FLAVORFUL FILL

Christmas is the perfect time for stuffing and getting some juicy breasts with this hand job! But before you dig in, let's make sure you've got your technique down. Start by prepping your stuffing and spread the legs open. Thoroughly stuff it inside the opening of your turkey. Tye the legs together to keep the inside moist, but don't play with your meat too much! Whether you're craving light meat or dark, all will be moist with patience and good technique. As you gather around the terrific spread, undo those pants and enjoy—everyone will be ready to burst!

Looking for Hooters

SNEAK A PEEK AT TOP-HEAVY TWEETS

Ready to go on a wild hunt this winter? Bird-watching is the best way to see hooters in the wild! While many chicks fly south, some colorful birds firmly stick around in the cold. Grab your binoculars with this hand job and get those beauties right up in your face! Whether you prefer small, delicate pairs or big, attention-grabbing ones, the thrill is in spotting them all. There's nothing quite like seeing natural ones in their element. So bundle up, adjust your focus, and enjoy up-close and personal views of nature's finest hooters.

Empty Your Sack

THE MOST WISHED-FOR GIFTS COME AT NIGHT

He's the jolly old man who only comes once a year, but when he does, it's a banger! Sliding down chimneys with rosy red cheeks and a bulging sack just begging to be emptied. Santa's all about blowing his load on presents for those who managed to stay off the naughty list. Sometimes, with this hand job, he gets jammed in the chimney, but fear not, he never slips in through the back door. Remember, it's crucial to keep your presents snugly wrapped under the tree, or you might find yourself in a sticky situation quicker than you can say, "Ho ho ho!"

Pound Your Dough

BEAT, AND REPEAT... FOR A TASTY TREAT

Ready to get down and dirty with some holiday sweets? Whipping up cookies is a seasonal hand job, and nothing beats the thrill of pounding that dough! With flour, eggs, sugar, and a splash of vanilla for a hint of spice, it's fun to get messy with friends. Sampling the goods before it's baked is part of the pleasure, especially when it's raw! Things can get sticky, so keep a towel ready to clean up the aftermath. And don't forget to give your beater and tools a good wash once you're done scrambling and kneading. Fresh from the oven, these treats are piping hot, gooey, and ready to taste!

Getting Horny

GET CRAFTY FOR THE PERFECT NIGHTCAP

Ready to get into the holiday spirit and get a little horny? Get touchy with this hand job by making pointy Santa Claus hats! Grab red fabric, needle, thread, and fluffy white balls. With a bit of creativity and some subtle handwork, stick your needle in and out with care. Your final creation should hang flaccid, with the balls draped perfectly over the side. To turn heads, fondle the point so it lays just right, making sure it doesn't droop too far over your face. Don't worry—the result will have everyone blushing as you deck their halls with hats with fluffy balls.

Stocking Stuffing

FILL YOUR SPOT WITH A SEASONAL SURPRISE

Nothing says Christmas like a well-stuffed stocking! These warm pockets are practically begging to be filled, and it's always stimulating to discover the oral delights nestled in your private stash. With this hand job, shove it in, but be gentle! You don't want to damage the tender velvet lining. Whether you're slipping in tantalizing treats or packing in something extra special, there's a particular thrill in seeing your stocking swell into a firm and impressive shape, making all your friends green with sock envy.

Blow Your Load

CLEAR A PATH FOR WINTER'S WHITE WONDERS

Ready to blow your load this winter? Whether you're tackling the front or aiming to clear the back, snow-blowing is an art form. This hand job demands savvy maneuvers, so wear protection to shield your parts from the elements. Sure, you can labor manually, but the automatic option finishes faster and offers more horsepower. With a powerful thrust, push your snow blower over the pathways. You know it's working when the machine shoots a white blast, carving a clear path and wowing onlookers.

Tap That Ass

BRING THE PARTY TO THE BACK

Create a party that slaps this holiday season by playing "Pin the Tail on the Donkey!" Start this classic hand job by hanging a picture of a jolly rump on the wall and pick up a tail! Now comes the fun part: tap that ass by getting that tail into the right spot! This game is no fun without a blindfold, so, cover those peepers, get handsy, and compete to nail that backside. The closest wins ultimate bragging rights: getting some quality tail!

Call Some Hookers

GET YOUR MOTOR RUNNING WITH A HOOKUP

Occasionally, during the holidays, your main ride just won't start. It's time to call a tow truck for help with this hand job! Sometimes the old banger just needs a little charge of the batteries and sometimes it is completely broken down from the cold. Not to worry, a good mechanic can either repair your car, or pull up the old hooker to tow that beauty back to the shop to look under the hood. This is nothing to be ashamed of. Every good provider needs a good hooker on speed dial!

Jingle Bells

GRAB EM' AND SPREAD SOME JINGLE JOY

Ready to get festive with your shiny balls of joy? It's all about the right touch and the perfect fondle with this hand job. Bigger ones usually jingle a bit lower, and shaking them just right will let everyone know you're coming on your sleigh from a mile away. But be careful—not too much shaking, or things might go south! Give them a gentle jiggle to spread holiday cheer and some impressive Ho-Ho-Hos!

Cream Pie

A DELICIOUS TREAT YOU NEVER SAW COMING!

What is this creamy dessert? Your auntie said she asked the baker man, and he filled her in! First, he said, come prepared by making the custard. Begin mixing sugar, milk, and cornstarch. Mix in eggs at the end, but don't do so prematurely, or things will fall flat! Squirt the custard it into a flaky crust, and bam! You've conceived the perfect climax to any dinner party!

BONUS CONTENT FROM VOLUME 2

Bust a Nut

GET OFF AND OUT OF THAT SHELL!

Some foods have a hard shell that you need to remove to eat what's inside. That's okay! This hand job is easy! Just grab your favorite nuts, a nutcracker, and your hands. Put the nut in the nutcracker's mouth and pull the lever. Smash! You just busted a nut! Now, you can put the tasty goodness in your mouth! But don't be greedy! Save some busted nuts for others. Remember to be careful as some people are allergic!

BONUS CONTENT
FROM VOLUME 1

Remember Kids...

THE BEST WAY TO SPREAD HOLIDAY JOY IS BY LENDING A <u>HELPING HAND</u>!

The End

THIS STORY HAS A HAPPY ENDING...
GRAB THE REST AND NEVER HAVE IDLE HANDS AGAIN!

SCAN
FOR THE WHOLE
FAMILY PACKAGE!

COLLECT THEM ALL!

Hey Legend!

LIKE FREE STUFF?
WE'VE GOT YOU COVERED!

We at Cleveland Steamer Press can't thank you enough for picking up this book and making it all the way through. Hopefully, you didn't disrupt any birthday parties or religious gatherings along the way—or did you?

As a token of our appreciation, we'd love to give you a free book on us. Scan the QR code to the right to claim yours and keep the good times rolling.

We hope you enjoyed this book, and thank you again for supporting independent publishing. If you're interested in our other titles, please visit our website: www.clevelandsteamerpress.com

From our family to yours,
The Cleveland Steamer Press Crew

Get a Free Book!

SCAN TO GET A FREE COPY OF ONE OF
OUR CRITICALLY DISDAINED BOOKS!

www.ingramcontent.com/pod-product-compliance
Lightning Source LLC
Chambersburg PA
CBHW041155120626
46547CB00020B/3226